Praise for True

"Rather than throw up his hands in despair over grid-lock and extreme partisan politics in Washington, Ted Wachtel offers a solution that can save our democracy by highlighting a time-tested method that is simple as it is sensible. Very thoughtful and persuasive."
 – *Phil Goldsmith, former CEO of the School District of Philadelphia and former Deputy Mayor and City Manager of Philadelphia*

"True Representation of the democratic spirit has been Ted Wachtel's ambition and contribution for all his life. This book shows the sad predicament of citizen cynicism about our democracies. Institutional renewal is required, and a book with clarity of thought about that renewal is needed. Here is that book. It explores practical ideas for a more deliberative democracy that can deliver better government, and government that richly engages the hearts and minds of citizens."
 – *John Braithwaite, Distinguished Professor at Australia National University and founder of the Regulatory Institutions Network*

"Wachtel provides compelling evidence that democracies can and should become more representative. Learning from others, we don't have to be complacent or reinvent the wheel. We simply have to be willing to challenge ourselves and take small steps."
 – *Linda Kligman, Vice President for Administration, IIRP Graduate School*

"As a conservative, I consider myself to be a strong constitutionalist, but part of that document's genius is the amendment process. In this book, Ted Wachtel advocates an audacious change in our governmental system, using 'sortition': basically a lottery process, such as that used in the selection of jurors in the criminal justice system. Given the convergence of soaring governmental debt, an impending entitlement disaster, and increasing partisan polarization and gridlock, it could well be time to give the idea of sortition serious consideration. I applaud Ted Wachtel for his efforts to bring the concept to the forefront of public discussion."
— *Jim Roberts, President, Radio America*

"Our current political system is an example of insanity— repeatedly doing the same thing that doesn't work— while expecting different results. Working with two different manufacturers, I experienced the benefit of replacing an inward-looking system of evaluation with a customer-defined value system. That is what True Representation can do for our democracies."
— *Bill Ballantine, former Human Resources Manager and former Republican Committeeman*

"True Representation is more than a modern manifesto for our times. It is a think-and-do book that provides a succinct, logical framework that makes meaningful and sustainable change possible in our lifetime. Whether you live in Boise or Belfast, the existing forms of democratic elections and governance aren't working. Ted Wachtel puts both power and responsibility back into the hands of the people, where it belongs."
— *Kerra L. Bolton, CNN Op-Ed Contributor and former Director of Communications, Outreach and Oppositional Research for the North Carolina Democratic Party*

Other books by Ted Wachtel

Author
Beyond the Schoolhouse:
Learning For A New Reality

Dreaming of a New Reality:
How restorative practices reduce crime and violence,
improve relationships and strengthen civil society

Real Justice:
How We Can Revolutionize Our Response To Wrongdoing

The Electronic Congress:
A Blueprint for Participatory Democracy

Co-Author
Toughlove

Toughlove Solutions

The Restorative Practices Handbook
for Teachers, Disciplinarians and Administrators

Restorative Circles in Schools:
Building Community and Enhanced Learning

Restorative Justice Conferencing:
RealJustice© and the Conferencing Handbook

Family Power:
Engaging and Collaborating With Families

Building Campus Community:
Restorative Practices in Residential Life

Editor
Safer Saner Schools: Restorative Practices in Education

True Representation

◆◆

How Citizens' Assemblies and Sortition Will Save Democracy

by

Ted Wachtel

published by

THE PIPER'S PRESS
Pipersville, Pennsylvania • USA

TRUE REPRESENTATION: How CITIZENS' ASSEMBLIES AND SORTITION WILL SAVE DEMOCRACY

Copyright © 2020 The Piper's Press
All Rights Reserved

FIRST EDITION

THE PIPER'S PRESS
P.O. Box 400
Pipersville, PA 18947 USA

Edited by
Mary Shafer

BuildingANewReality.com Book Series
PRINT ISBN 978-1-934355-45-9
EBOOK ISBN 978-1-934355-46-6

PRINTED IN THE U.S.A.

True Representation is the key goal of representative governance — the bullseye of democracy.

– *Ted Wachtel*

Table of Contents

CHAPTER 1

What To Do
For Your Country

On October 28, 1960, when I was fourteen, I watched John F. Kennedy speak to tens of thousands of people assembled[1] in the square and side streets around the Soldiers and Sailors Monument in the center of Allentown, Pennsylvania. I was looking down from a window several stories above Kennedy, in the old YMCA building, having been recruited by a high school friend to dump boxes of confetti, which fluttered down to the speakers' platform below. That day, Kennedy became my hero.

Three months later, on January 20, 1961, I hung on every word of his inaugural address (written by Ted Sorenson, one of the most inspirational presidential speechwriters ever). When Kennedy proclaimed, "Ask not what your country can do for you, ask what you can do for your country," his sentence penetrated my psyche and defined much of my motivation for the rest of my life.

John T. Gross,[2] who was mayor of Allentown at the time, introduced Kennedy to the crowd. A couple of years later, Mayor Gross introduced me to a much smaller crowd when I cut the ribbon to re-open a newly renovated department store, just a block from the spot where Kennedy had stood. I had been elected student "Mayor for the Day" and spent the day accompanying the mayor.

I wondered if I, too, could become president. During my fledgling political career, I was elected president of my local youth group, high school senior class officer and president of my college residence hall. I took advantage of every experience that would teach me about the art of politics.

But I became disillusioned. I remember walking into my high school guidance counselor's office where everyone was gathered around a small television, to find out that President Kennedy was dead. The succession of violence stunned me: Robert F. Kennedy, Malcom X, Martin Luther King, Vietnam, Kent State and Jackson State cast a long shadow on my spirit.

My most important realization, however, came from a definition in the very first chapter of my first political science textbook. It challenged my naive notions when it bluntly stated that, "politics is the pursuit of power."

It said nothing about altruism nor "what you can do for your country," nor truth, justice and the American way. The more I delved into history and politics, the more I realized that I couldn't do what politicians have to do to win elections, so I abandoned my political aspirations.

The Search for Good Governance

But I was still deeply concerned about good governance. As a young couple, my wife, Susan, and I became a committee-woman and committeeman in our small town. We campaigned for people we cared about, but couldn't bring ourselves to back some of our party's candidates who were nothing more than political hacks.

In 1972, handing out McGovern[3] literature at a supermarket in our largely conservative community, Susan, six months pregnant, came face-to-face with how politics brings out the worst in people. She was assailed by Nixon supporters who told her that "people like you don't belong here." She held her ground, insisting, "This isn't Nazi Germany. I have every right to be here." Her assailants retreated when I happened to arrive at the supermarket with a newspaper photographer.

We both dabbled in political campaigns for a while, but became increasingly disenchanted with the motives of many of the candidates we met. Susan still does phone calls and puts up signs for an occasional candidate she particularly likes, but I found myself searching for other ways to "do for my country."

Rearranging the Deck Chairs

In 1975, I was working on my doctorate in Educational Media and looking for an interesting project for my dissertation. I got interested in a local government reform effort called the Bucks County Home Rule Charter Commission. The Commission proposed a change in the structure of county government in hopes of improving it, but they had to sell it to the voters in a referendum.

I produced an audiovisual production for the Home Rule Charter Commission as part of my doctoral dissertation. I hoped that my educational slide and sound production would more effectively inform the voters. My hypothesis was that if we improved the quality of information and its delivery, using educational media, we could improve public decision-making.

I drove around the county to innumerable meetings. People said they loved my sound-slide show and especially the rendition of *Yankee Doodle*[4] that I used in the soundtrack, but in the end most people decided how to vote on the basis of political party. The Republicans, who were dominant in Bucks County, Pennsylvania, voted against change, and the Democrats, who wanted to become dominant, not surprisingly, voted for change.

The notion of structural reform failed to deal with the underlying problem of democratic decision-making: the inability of the public to make informed and thoughtful choices. In the end, I realized that reforms like the Home Rule Charter Commission are as likely to save democracy as rearranging the deck chairs would have saved the Titanic.

The Electronic Congress

In my next experiment in improving governance, in 1992, I wrote and published a book called *The Electronic Congress: A Blueprint for Democracy.*[5] At the time, independent presidential candidate Ross Perot had suggested an at-home computerized referendum mechanism, so that the citizenry could vote on legislation proposed by a commission of experts. Perot's idea was criticized for bypassing the checks and balances of a bicameral legislature, raising fears that American founder James Madison's nightmare of mob rule would come true.

Instead, my book proposed an approach to national referenda that I hoped would address that concern, by relying on Congress to propose issues for national referenda by telephone voting, which would allow people to consider and vote for issues separately from the hustle and bustle of candidates' political campaigns and election day.

But talk is cheap and without action means little. I have been profoundly influenced by the late Buckminster Fuller,[6] one of the 20th century's great innovators, who said: "You never change things by fighting the existing reality. To change something, build a new model that makes the existing model obsolete." With each of the dozen or so books[7] that I have written or edited,

I have always built a working model or I have already been operating a project or program related to the content of the book.

Simultaneous with the publication of my book, I also launched the Telephone Referendum Project as a small experimental model of the Electronic Congress. People who enrolled could respond to a written bulletin mailed to them, posing several questions related to summarized national issues, by phoning in their votes to an 800 number.

My wife's voice, digitized by a computer programmer, guided callers through the voting process. Most of the participants had purchased my book, or were college students assigned by their professors to participate, or had read about my experiment in a cooperating newspaper in Nebraska. I had fun running the project for a couple of years and learned a lot, mostly from my mistakes.

In the process of researching the *Electronic Congress* book, I delved into the history and contemporary use of referenda. I have since come to realize that the limitations in referenda are the same as the limitations of public-opinion polling[8] (discussed in more detail later) and elections:

- *Rational ignorance*—People think their vote is too insignificant to invest time in studying the issues.
- *Non-existent opinions*—Voters often just make random decisions when they're uninformed.
- *Insular opinions*—Many people merely reflect

the opinions of their own social group without considering other perspectives.

Moreover, the huge amount of money that special interests spend to support or defeat referenda replicates the problems of elections. Media campaigns routinely employ negative advertising that distorts, exaggerates and lies, hoping to raise doubts among the uninformed. Referenda are no better than elections or structural reform. They still do not deal with the underlying problem of democracy—citizens who vote without knowing enough to make good decisions, and politicians who are willing to exploit their ignorance.

CHAPTER **2**

The Myth of Voting

Most people believe that voting is democracy, and that an election is the only democratic way to choose people for public office. But they are mistaken.

The American Civil Liberties Union and the United Nations refer to voting as the "cornerstone of our liberty"[9] and the "crux of democracy." But they are mistaken.

The original democracy[10] in ancient Athens, Greece chose only ten percent of its public officials by election, selecting the rest by sortition[11]—a lottery which randomly selected citizens to serve as legislators, jurors, magistrates and administrators. They used a randomization device called a *kleroterion*[12] to choose the names of those who would serve.

American and British courts have carried on the Athenian

tradition of sortition for hundreds of years, selecting jury members randomly from lists of taxpayers, voters or registered drivers. No less important than legislatures, we trust juries with our most momentous decisions—whether to take freedom or even life itself from our fellow human beings.

Representative democracies that preceded the founding of the American republic, from Athens to Italian city states, used sortition to choose most officeholders, rather than elections.

At first everyone laughs at the idea of randomly selecting our legislators by lottery. Yet everyone agrees that our legislators are critically compromised by their need to beg for election campaign donations.

So, why the laughter?

When public officials accept donations, they make themselves vulnerable to the demands of donors. They struggle to follow their own consciences. As an influential Congressional lobbyist once quipped, most legislators "would like to do the right thing, if only they could get away with it."[13]

Numbers Don't Lie

Aristotle, the Athenian philosopher, wrote, "The appointment of magistrates by lot is thought to be democratic, and the election of them oligarchic."[14] Sortition is the best method of choosing officeholders in a democracy because with selection by lot, statistical probability guarantees that those chosen truly represent the citizenry (explained below). Election is best to sustain an oligarchy because wealthy, powerful individuals can readily manipulate the election process. Sortition hits the bulls-eye of democratic governance. Every citizen, stockholder or member would be more truly represented, in governments, corporations and membership organizations, if their legislatures and boards of directors were selected at random from among their constituents.

Just as in public opinion polls, the larger the sample size selected, the lower the margin of error. A larger sample more accurately reflects everything about the target population—from attitudes and opinions to physical traits like age, left-handedness or hair color.

Democracy Distorted

In our current reality, powerful individuals and organizations distort the democratic process in countries around the world by:

. giving large donations of money or human resources to political campaigns

. promising lucrative jobs to public officials after they leave office, or

. bribing officials with cash, travel and gifts while in office.

Around the globe, supposedly, democracy won.

Most countries in the world claim to be democracies. Even North Korea, led by a third-generation dictator,[15] masquerades as the Democratic People's Republic of Korea.

Yet in a world once dominated by monarchs, money now rules. Longstanding democracies in the Americas and Europe have become so corrupt that they not only don't hit the bullseye of true representation, they miss the whole damn target. The democratic process is no longer a deliberation. It has become an auction, selling favors to the highest bidders.

Prudence

In 1776, a sentence in the Declaration of Independence noted: "Prudence, indeed, will dictate that Governments long established should not be changed for light and transient Causes."[16]

I wholeheartedly agree. Given how strange and new the whole idea of sortition is to all of us, we should proceed thoughtfully and evaluate each step. But to do nothing about elections leaves us stuck in the corrupt world that democracies now inhabit, dominated by party politicians who are beholden to the wealthy and the powerful. While we have made many attempts at campaign finance reform, it's proved to be as successful as asking a fox to guard the henhouse.

The cynicism about democracy in my own country, the United States, and elsewhere, has grown to the point that:

. In the United States, more than 40 percent of eligible voters don't vote in presidential elections.

. Usually more than 60 percent don't vote in

mid-term elections. (More than 50 percent in the 2018 election.)

- Over 70 percent don't vote in presidential primary elections.
- Over 60 percent don't vote in state and local elections.
- Nearly 80 percent don't vote in state and local primary elections.

Voting in elections is also declining in European Parliament[17] elections, in European countries and around the globe.[18] Increasingly, people do not trust their elected representatives to speak the truth. Politicians in democracies around the world have sacrificed truth on the altar of power. Truth has become irrelevant. Winning elections is all that matters.

Citizens see their elected representatives as primarily concerned with enriching themselves. A Transparency International survey[19] of 114,000 people in 107 countries found that, in the most recent survey, only 30 percent believed their governments were effectively dealing with corruption.

In the late 1950s, about 75 percent of Americans expressed trust in their country's government "most or all of the time." Now only 19 percent of Americans trust their government "most or all of the time."[20]

These are not "light and transient Causes." They are as significant as the "Causes" that provoked the American colonists in 1776 to rise up in violent revolution against their king, and create a new form of government—a democratic republic that has helped to inspire the birth of other democratic republics around the world.

However, when Benjamin Franklin, one of the founders of the American republic, emerged from Independence Hall in Philadelphia after the secret deliberations of the Constitutional Convention of 1787, he was asked by Mrs. Elizabeth Powel, who was in the crowd outside the hall, "Well, Doctor, what have we got—a republic or a monarchy?"

Franklin responded, "A republic, madam, if you can keep it."[21]

What Can We Do?

We must build a new reality for democracy. However, we do not need violent revolutions with blood and tears. The citizens of most democracies still have at their disposal the ability to make change through voting, but the challenge is to get people focused and mobilized to use that power effectively. That is the purpose of this manifesto.[22]

We aim to redefine how governance is done, creating local, state, regional and national "citizens' assemblies,"[23] whether official or experimental, whose members are selected by sortition. We will demonstrate that, under the right conditions (which I'll discuss later), large groups of ordinary citizens can make thoughtful, informed decisions about complex problems—as well as or better than legislators whose decisions are tainted by their desire to get re-elected.

James Fishkin,[24] founder of Stanford University's Center for

Deliberative Democracy,[25] established Deliberative Polling™ as the gold standard for citizens' assemblies by extensively researching "the right conditions."

In 1996-1998, he organized eight regional assemblies in Texas.[26] These citizens of the so-called "gas and oil state," after thoughtful consideration, came out so strongly for renewable energy that Texas has since moved from the 49th state to number one in renewable energy production. In 2011, a three-day assembly of 412 Californians demonstrated how ordinary citizens can make thoughtful decisions about a wide range of complex issues, from taxation to electoral reform. (See *What's Next California*,[27] a one-hour PBS television special.)

The U.K.'s Sortition Foundation[28] advocates replacing the British House of Lords[29] with a "House of Citizens," so that the elected House of Commons[30] could not pass legislation without the consent of a statistically representative group of citizens in a second legislature. The Foundation has recently finalized its strategy document, outlining a three-phase process to radically transform democracy to what they call "Sortition Democracy."

Phase 1

Regular Sortition Assemblies

Phase 2

Instituted Sortition Assembly or Chamber

Phase 3

Sortition Democracy

According to Brett Hennig,[31] director of the Sortition Foundation, Phase 1 is well underway in many other countries around the world. He says there is evidence that Phase 2 may also be fast approaching.

Phase 1

The earliest government-sponsored assemblies were only advisory. In 2004 and 2006, British Columbia and Ontario, Canada, and the Netherlands used citizens' assemblies[32] to deal with questions of electoral system reform. A quasi-random process was used to guarantee accurate geographic and demographic distribution. Participants were provided with an introductory course in electoral politics. Then they reviewed and deliberated about alternative proposals for electoral reform and made recommendations.

Belgium pioneered the first large-scale citizens' assembly in Europe. In November, 2011, frustrated by the record-breaking political impasse in which Belgium's two leading political parties took 589 days to form a government, private Belgian citizens acted on their own. They organized a national G1000,[33] their name for a large experimental Citizens' Summit that deliberated and identified key issues of concern for Belgians. Since then, the Dutch have used the G1000 concept to organize local citizens' assemblies. The U.K. is currently sponsoring several advisory citizens' assemblies, selected by sortition, to make recommendations about social care and various local or regional issues.

In his blogpost[34] for my Building A New Reality[35] website, Brett Hennig explains how, "Over the course of 18 months, from October 2016 to April 2018, ninety-nine randomly selected Irish citizens did an incredible thing: they made policy recommendations to their government. And what's more, the government listened and responded.

"The most well-known proposal put forth by this Irish Citizens' Assembly[36] (see documentary film[37]) was that the Irish constitutional ban on abortion be removed. The resulting referendum, in May, 2018, did just that. Now the government is turning its attention to another set of recommendations coming from the citizens' assembly: how to make Ireland a leader in tackling climate change.

"Citizens' Assemblies are growing in popularity for several reasons, not least of which is that people trust them, whereas people don't trust politicians. A second principal reason is that, for politicians, assemblies open up a political space for controversial issues to be tackled in a non-partisan way—their legitimacy stems from the fact that they honor the informed decision of a representative group of citizens. Very few politicians wanted to talk about abortion publicly in Ireland before it went on the

Citizens' Assembly agenda. After the assembly's deliberations you could hardly stop them."

Phase 2

However, recent developments are trending from advisory toward authority—giving assemblies the power to make legally binding decisions, rather than recommendations. Since 2016, Gdansk, Poland, has delegated municipal authority[38] to its citizenry by convening a series of assemblies that meet for several days on a specific issue. Approximately sixty citizens are randomly selected for several days to hear testimony from experts, ask questions and deliberate in small groups, and then render a binding policy decision. (Tragically, the man responsible for this democratic innovation, Gdansk's popular mayor, Pawel Adamowicz,[39] was assassinated on January 14, 2019.)

A regional parliament in Belgium plans to complement their single-chamber legislature with a second permanent sortition body. Similarly, Madrid, Spain intends to create a bicameral city council, with a second council chamber selected by sortition.

Phase 3

Brett Hennig is optimistic. He asserts that "electoral party politics is broken and dysfunctional. Everyone knows that. But now there is hope...When a critical mass of people and communities have experienced or heard about the benefits of sortition it will be time to move to the national stage and transform our broken democracies—bringing about The End of Politicians[40] (Hennig's book) and the beginning of a real democracy of, by and for the people."

CHAPTER 3

The Wisdom
of Crowds

James Surowiecki[41] wrote the book on large group decision-making. In *The Wisdom of Crowds*,[42] he argues that large groups of ordinary people, given the right conditions, make better decisions than experts. His book was named the "best business book of 2004" by both *Businessweek* and *Forbes*.

He begins his book with the amazing story of British scientist Francis Galton,[43] himself an elitist, who in 1906 discovered "the wisdom of crowds" at a country fair contest in which individuals tried to guess the weight of an ox. No one's guess, no matter how expert that person might be, was as accurate as the collective guess of the crowd. The average of the 787 guesses proved to be perfect. The ox weighed exactly 1198 pounds. Galton's remarkable discovery contradicted popular assumptions that human groups are like herds, easily influenced and likely to make rash, emotional decisions.

James Madison's Nightmare

But in 1787, those who wrote the American Constitution had doubts about the wisdom of crowds. The founders created an "Electoral College"[44] to select the president and vice-president. Until 1913, when the 17th Amendment changed the Constitution, Senators were elected by state legislatures, not voters.

Constitutional scholar Jeffrey Rosen[45] describes the founders' thinking: "The Senate would comprise natural aristocrats chosen by state legislators rather than elected by the people. And rather than directly electing the chief executive, the people would vote for wise electors—that is, propertied white men—who would ultimately choose a president of the highest character and most discerning judgment."

James Madison,[46] known as the Father of the Constitution, arrived for the Constitutional Convention in Philadelphia in 1787[47] with two trunks full of history books about how previous democracies failed.

Rather than a direct democracy, the founders created a representative republic. Madison saw the Senate as a "necessary fence" against the "fickleness and passion" of the citizenry and the members of the House of Representatives, whom they elected. George Washington said that the framers of the Constitution had created the Senate to "cool" House legislation,[48] just as a saucer was used to cool hot tea.

Madison and the other founders were determined to avoid the mistakes of the past, but as the title of Rosen's article in the October 2018 issue of *The Atlantic* proclaims, "America is Living James Madison's Nightmare."[49]

The founders could not have anticipated the unintended consequences of ignoring the original democratic tradition of sortition. Instead they relied on competitive elections to choose decision-makers—except for choosing jurors for the court system by lottery. Now, more than two centuries later, competitive elections have devolved into trials by combat, in which candidates for public office beat each other up in debates and with negative attack ads that exaggerate, distort and straight-out lie.

The Human Race as Supercomputer

Surowiecki's remarkable story of the crowd at a 1906 country fair—who collectively guessed the weight of an ox—suggests that it's as if we human beings can be wired together like small computers, to collectively achieve the intelligence of a supercomputer. If we collate all the individual decisions of a great many human beings, we integrate their strengths, weaknesses and diverse opinions to achieve a far more accurate composite perspective than that of any individual expert.

That's the principle underlying stock index funds,[50] which are a composite of the decisions of all of the people buying stocks listed in a particular index. Every year, the index funds beat more than half of the stock funds managed by expert stock-pickers. Every year.

It's also the principle underlying the remarkable fact that the average of a group of individuals guessing the number of jelly beans in a jar will get closer to the correct total than any individual guess. Routinely.

Finding a Missing Submarine

The most astounding example of the wisdom of crowds is the process that naval officer John Craven used to find a submarine after it suddenly disappeared in the North Atlantic in May, 1968. Although the sub's last reported location was known, no one knew how far it might have traveled after its last radio contact. The designated search area was a circle twenty miles wide and thousands of feet deep.

Craven assembled a group with varied backgrounds, including submarine experts, mathematicians and salvage men, asking them not to consult one another. Then he offered each of them a series of alternative explanations for what might have happened to the U.S.S. Scorpion. He asked each of them to offer his best guess as to its exact location. Finally, he employed a formula called Bayes' theorem, which is a way of calculating how new information about an event changes the pre-existing expectations.

When he was done, Craven had what was, roughly speaking, the group's collective estimate of where the submarine was located. No individual member of the group picked that location, but it was the collective judgment of the group as a whole.

Five months after the Scorpion disappeared, a navy ship found the submarine 220 yards from where Craven's group had said it would be.

The Right Conditions for Good Group Decision-Making

Why don't our legislatures work like the founders intended? Because they cannot satisfy James Surowiecki's five conditions for good group decision-making.

Let's go down the checklist. There are two preconditions:

1. The group must have an agreed-upon mechanism for turning their private judgments into a collective decision of the group. Yes, our legislatures have those voting mechanisms in place—but political parties routinely squabble about legislative procedure, changing or bending the legislative rules for strategic advantage. They cannot even agree upon the election process itself, arguing about technical issues like Palm Beach County's ballot problems[51] in the 2000 presidential election, or attempts by Republicans to change voter registration requirements that Democrats claim disadvantage their constituents. No, our legislatures do not have an agreed-upon mechanism.

2. The group must have timely access to good information. Yes, legislatures can call upon official agencies to provide information—but the current divisive U.S. political climate has made that more complicated. In the era of "fake news,"[52] some legislators not only doubt reputable mainstream media, but have cast doubt on non-partisan information, such as financial projections from their own GAO (Government Accountability Office) and conclusions made by their own intelligence agencies and the FBI. No, our legislatures can't even agree on what is good information.

Most importantly, Surowiecki defines three other conditions for an intelligent large group decision-making process. The group must have:

. diversity of opinion

. independence of judgment, and

. decentralized decision-making.

Let's see if our U.S. Congress or state legislatures can meet those three critical conditions:

Diversity of opinion. The average state legislator in the United States is a white male Protestant in his sixties, with a graduate degree and a business background. In the current U.S. Congress, more than half of all Senators and more than a third of all Representatives are lawyers. No, our state and national legislatures lack the diversity of perspective that comes from people of varied age, gender, occupation, income, religious belief and ethnicity.

Independence of Judgment. In every legislative body in America, there is a specialized party official called "the whip," whose job is to keep individual legislators from exercising their own judgment and straying from their political party's position on any issue. They are even authorized to threaten lawmakers with the loss of campaign funding in the next election. No, our legislators are constrained from voting independently by their political parties.

Decentralized Decision-making. Political parties hold caucuses to keep tabs on their own members. Party leaders carefully hand out committee assignments to legislators who will enforce decision-making along party lines. No, our legislatures do not decentralize decision-making.

The simple and sad truth is that the leaders of political parties cannot allow the right conditions for good group decision-making. Diversity, independence and decentralization jeopardize their control of the legislative machinery, and the financial rewards it brings them. Because of the combative, costly and corrupt election process we use to select our decision-makers, we fail to achieve true representation.

Sortition and Surowiecki's Five Conditions
Whether we use sortition to choose:
. members of all legislatures, or
. members for one house of a bicameral legislature, or
. the participants in single-issue citizens' assemblies,

randomly selected groups readily meet Surowiecki's five conditions for good large group decision-making.

Because the sole purpose of a political party is to win elections, if we chose legislators by sortition instead of election, we would shrink the need for political parties and thereby minimize their influence. There would be no professional politicians serving term after term. There would be no one buying influence with campaign donations, because there would be no campaigns. There would be no attack ads, name-calling and nasty accusations.

Without the squabbling of politicians seeking advantage over their rivals, it should be relatively easy to achieve an agreed-upon mechanism for turning private judgments into a collective decision and to establish timely access to good information. There is no incentive to fight about voter identification, limiting the hours and number of polling places, or the validity of information from reliable private and public sources.

Sortition would dramatically improve the diversity of a legislature. For example, if the 100 U.S. Senators were selected by lottery from the U.S. population, the make-up of the Senate would change dramatically to approximately fifty percent men and fifty percent women and a wide range of ethnicities and occupations. For example, in the random sample shown in the graphic (next page), 51 women and 49 men were selected. The larger the sample size, the smaller the margin of error.[53]

The graphic on the next page, created by Zach Roberts, shows the contrast between the gender, age and ethnic diversity of U.S. Senators as if they were selected by lottery, versus the current majority of predominately older white men who comprise the U.S. Senate. (See the interactive version,[54] which allows your computer's cursor to hover over the graphs for more detailed information.)

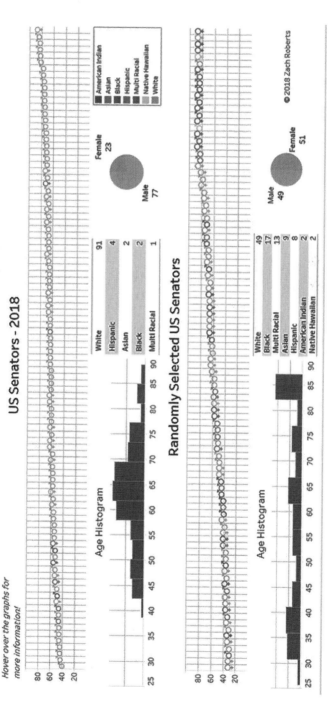

© 2018 Zach Roberts

As for improving independence of judgment and decentralized decision-making, without the party majority and minority committee chairs and party whips enforcing the party line, legislators would be free to vote their consciences and to actually represent the desires of their constituents.

Afterword

In the Afterword of a later edition of his book, James Surowiecki describes how people wanted to test the hypothesis of *The Wisdom of Crowds* whenever he made public appearances. Not just by having the group guess the number of jellybeans in a jar, but with stranger challenges like trying to guess the number of books in James Surowiecki's home library. He was surprised because he didn't know the number of books himself, but he described the setting where he shelved his books to provide basic information. He worried on each occasion that the wisdom of crowds wouldn't work, that the group's average guess might not be better than that of individuals. But it was. Reliably.

CHAPTER 4

The Nation In
A Room

George Gallup,[55] the pioneering American pollster, asserted in his 1940 book, *The Pulse of Democracy*,[56] that modern public opinion polling would replicate the New England town meeting on a national scale. He said that, "The newspapers and the radio conduct the debate on national issues...just as the townsfolk did in person in the old town meeting." And then, through polls, "the people, having heard the debate on both sides of every issue, can express their will." It would be as if "the nation is literally in one great room."

Three Critical Limitations
As James Fishkin[57] explained in his 2006 article, "The Nation in a Room,"[58] Gallup's vision of reliable public-opinion polling suffers from three critical limitations:

. rational ignorance

. non-existent opinions, and

. insular opinions.

Rational ignorance is based on a perfectly rational concern: "Why should I spend a lot of time on complex policy issues when my vote is merely one among millions and won't make any significant difference?" Most people, faced with the realities of work, kids and a limited amount of leisure time, simply lack the incentive to learn and think about public policy issues.

Non-existent opinions can be explained by the fact that many respondents don't like to say, "I don't know." Instead, they often pick an answer at random, skewing the results of a poll due to embarrassment at their lack of knowledge.

Insular opinions are formed in a bubble, in which respondents merely reflect the opinions of people like themselves, who talk only to each other and pay attention only to the media that expresses their group's views. They are insulated from diverse information and perspectives.

So, why would we trust ordinary citizens, selected by sortition, to understand complex policy issues and be effective decision-makers? Because we have come to realize, thanks to James Surowiecki and James Fishkin, that large groups of ordinary people can make good decisions under the right conditions.

Democracy When the People Are Thinking

In his 2018 book, *Democracy When the People Are Thinking: Revitalizing Our Politics Through Public Deliberation,*[59] James

Fishkin points to his more than 100 citizen assemblies in 28 countries that demonstrate exactly that potential. Called "Deliberative Polling™," his process is different from traditional polls that ask unprepared citizens to respond to issues they may not understand or even recognize. Instead, people are brought together in person, from a random sample scientifically selected to reflect the target population.

Initially, they are polled by telephone on the issues they'll be facing, and then invited to participate in person. In advance of the event, they get a briefing book representing varied perspectives, with the opposing parties agreeing on the fairness of the briefing book before it is finalized. Over one or more days, people meet in large and small groups, hear experts with conflicting perspectives, ask questions, have discussions and ultimately respond to the same poll for a second time. An individual's choices are not revealed, only the overall outcomes.

Fishkin says, "The public is very smart if you give it a chance...If people think their voice actually matters, they'll do the hard work, really study their briefing books, ask the experts smart questions and then make tough decisions. When they hear the experts disagreeing, they're forced to think for themselves. About 70 percent change their minds in the process."

Funnily, a woman in the U.K., whose husband participated in a deliberative poll, told Fishkin that in their 30 years of marriage she had never seen her husband read a newspaper. However, after participating in the weekend of deliberation, she said, he now reads "every newspaper every day," and was "going to be much more interesting to live with in retirement."

Fishkin has found that when people have a reason to become informed, they give up their rational ignorance. He notes that, "Deliberation can change the habits of a lifetime. When we went back to the sample from the British event some 11 months later, we found that the participants were even more informed than they had been at the end of the weekend. Presumably, they continued to read newspapers and pay attention to the media, once activated by the intense discussions of a deliberative weekend."

For more than two decades, deliberative polling has tackled challenging issues, from energy needs planning in Texas to healthcare decisions in Italy, to closing segregated Roma schools in Bulgaria. Fishkin's projects persuasively demonstrate that ordinary citizens can deal with complex problems and make thoughtful decisions—free from the influence of money and the corruption of party politics.

A National Citizens' Assembly

So, what would it look like if the United States did something different? Perhaps we might create a one-time deliberative legislature as a demonstration project. There would be 435 representatives, one from each Congressional district, chosen by lottery.

It would be officially staffed and funded, and dedicated to deciding policy on a single controversial issue—like gun control—using Fishkin's deliberative polling process. Representatives and Senators and the President would voluntarily delegate their authority to this citizens' assembly.

There is little risk of diminishing respect for Congress by engaging in such an experiment. An overwhelming 76 percent of the public currently disapproves[60] of the way Congress is doing its job, an opinion that has persisted at that level or higher for most of the last decade.

There is historical precedent for voluntary delegation. The commission appointed in 2005 to deal with a controversial list of U.S. military base closings[61] only allowed Congress the option of a "yes" or "no" vote on the commission's proposed list. They were not allowed to offer amendments. So, an experimental one-time, single-issue citizens' assembly on gun control[62] could be created with a similar mandate. However, given the legitimacy of citizens' assemblies when compared to that of an appointed commission, we might reasonably ask our Senators and Representatives simply to ratify the decisions of a truly representative group of Americans, thoughtfully deliberating about a "hot potato" issue that politicians have avoided like the plague.

Most significantly, the single-issue citizens' assembly could do what never happens now. Instead of attacking the opposition in the usual adversarial brawl, members could:

. read briefing materials and hear presentations
  from lobbyists and other interested parties
. confer with knowledgeable experts and staff
. have a real conversation with one another
. and make thoughtful decisions.

What a radical idea: a deliberative body that actually deliberates—with decision-makers whose main concern is public policy, not fundraising and positioning themselves for the next election. Consider the comments of eight-term U.S. Congressman Steve Israel,[63] who decided not to run again. He said, "I don't think I can spend another day...begging for money. I always knew the system was dysfunctional. Now it is beyond broken."

The Irish Citizens' Assembly, whose authority to make decisions is based on voluntary delegation by the Irish legislature, live-streams and records all of its meetings, allowing their fellow citizens to observe the process. The delegates to the assembly spent five full weekends over five months, learning and deliberating about issues related to their constitution's total abortion ban, including testimony from women who had been affected. By the time they made their recommendations, they were more knowledgeable than almost anyone else in Ireland, including the members of their nation's legislature. Because they were selected by sortition, they were also more truly representative.

If the U.S. were to organize a similar assembly on gun control, for example, a one-time national citizens' assembly would not require a constitutional amendment—just a willingness on the part of Americans and their elected officials, like the Irish, to delegate Congressional authority to an experiment in participatory democracy. Substantial evidence and precedent all but guarantee a positive experience, a practical first step toward fulfilling George Gallup's hopeful vision of "the nation in a room."

CHAPTER 5

The Sortition Menu

We can use sortition at a national, state, or local level to choose:

- members of all legislatures or councils, or just one house of a bicameral legislature or council, or
- the members of single-issue citizens' assemblies, or
- jurors, or
- delegates to nominating assemblies and
- the Electoral College.

As we peruse the sortition menu, *let's allow ourselves to have fun and think creatively.* Our appetites may change after we've tasted all the main courses and an enticing dessert—a final section that may make the infamous Electoral College more palatable.

Legislatures and Councils

Brett Hennig's proposal, for a House of Citizens to replace the existing House of Lords in the United Kingdom, would use sortition to choose its members. They would serve full-time, receive salaries and have staff, just like the members of the House of Parliament, who would continue to be chosen in competitive elections.

Presumably, people who did not want to serve could refuse the opportunity. In a relatively small country like the U.K., distance from home would not be as significant a challenge as in a large country like the U.S. People's existing jobs would likely cause a problem, although short terms and substantial remuneration would help make the job more attractive. Further, laws similar to those protecting the jobs of Americans who serve in the National Guard for six months might provide a workable solution.

Also, good financial compensation and legal sanctions would be among the strategies to help ensure that participants do not take lucrative jobs or other kinds of bribes from those who want to influence legislation. There are other practical considerations that would need to be explored and decided, such as how to:

- insulate citizen legislators from undue influence by family, friends and others
- foster peer support to resist the pressures they face while serving
- take advantage of technologies to reduce the need for travel by supplementing face-to-face sessions with virtual meetings
- provide orientation for new members

- develop non-partisan civil service staff to frame briefing materials and write laws.

Rutgers University professor, Alex Guerrero,[64] in his 2014 journal article entitled "Against Elections: The Lottocratic Alternative,"[65] proposes an interesting approach to citizen legislatures. Instead of a traditional general legislature that deals with everything, he proposes a number of specialized legislatures to focus on different themes—agriculture, consumer protection, defense, education, environmental protection, financial services regulation, healthcare, tax policy. The narrower focus enables ordinary citizens to more easily learn what they need to know to thoughtfully legislate in a particular area of governance.

Guerrero recognizes that there could be many variations in this model, but he feels that the most critical element is the selection of legislators by lottery—a system of governance which he prefers to call "lottocracy."[66]

Guerrero favors random selection of legislators because: "In the presence of widespread citizen ignorance and the absence of meaningful accountability, powerful interests will effectively capture representatives, ensuring that the only viable candidates—the only people who can get and stay in political power—are those who will act in ways that are congenial to the interests of the powerful."

That sad reality was demonstrated in November, 2017, in the weeks before the vote approving the tax cut bill, which blatantly contradicted a traditional conservative concern about increasing the deficit. "My donors are basically saying, 'Get it done or don't ever call me again,'" said Representative Chris Collins.[67]

Senator Lindsey Graham admitted that if the GOP didn't pass the bill, "contributions will stop."

In the hours before the bill passed, Doug Deason, a Texas financier and major Republican donor, said, "It's just disappointing when you help put people in office and they don't do anything." (Please rest assured that donors are just as influential with Democrats.) In a lottocracy, legislators would be free to exercise their independent judgment and follow their own conscience.

Another distinctive feature of Guerrero's model is the structure. He suggests 300 legislators in each specialized legislature, who would be randomly selected for three-year terms, with 100 members retiring and 100 new members replacing them each year, just like the U.S. Senate that changes one-third of its members every two years. No need to add on the sweet icing of term limits—limits would already be baked into the cake.

The lottocratic alternative provides professional staff, including attorneys, who support each specialized legislature through a series of stages—agenda setting, expert presentations, consultation, deliberation, drafting, voting—in a process similar to Deliberative Polling; but it would last weeks or months, rather than just a weekend.

Single-Issue Citizens' Assemblies

If the first step the U.S. or any other country takes toward "True Representation"[68] is a one-time, single-issue citizens' assembly on a controversial issue like gun control, what would the next steps look like?

Perhaps a second and third and fourth citizens' assembly on climate change or abortion or immigration? Given the partisan gridlock that paralyzes Congress, we cannot count on today's politicians to deal with these urgent issues. They usually don't even give them a thoughtful discussion in the House or Senate. Most politicians are more concerned with getting re-elected than doing the right thing.

So, if our only use of sortition were to organize a series of national citizens' assemblies on challenging issues, with full-time legislators voluntarily delegating their authority, such as is happening now in Ireland, it would be a welcome improvement to our democracy. Critical issues that have languished for years without meaningful attention could move beyond the partisan gridlock of elected legislatures.

Jurors

As noted earlier, American and British courts have carried on the original Athenian tradition of selecting their jurors by sortition[69] for hundreds of years. A friend of mine wondered whether we could trust ordinary citizens, selected at random, with legislative decisions. When he was reminded that we trust ordinary citizens, randomly selected from lists of taxpayers, voters or registered drivers, to serve on juries, who have the authority to take freedom or even life itself from their fellow human beings, he said he needed no further convincing.

Delegates to Nominating Assemblies

No sooner does one election end, than politicians begin campaigning and seeking donations for the next one. Media pundits in print and on television hardly ever discuss issues, except in terms of how each issue will affect politicians' chances in the next election. Ironically, we invest far more time, money and energy choosing decision-makers than we spend on the decisions themselves.

Nominating assemblies could change all that. With delegates chosen by sortition, they could deliberate and choose officials like judges, mayors, governors and even presidents, on behalf of the citizenry that they truly represent.

Instead of primary elections and caucuses, nominating assemblies chosen by sortition could deliberate for a period of time, checking resumes, reading testimonials and interviewing their favored candidates. Then the assembly would recommend a slate of candidates for a final decision. This process would allow a candidate to reach the general election without a long and expensive campaign competing in primaries and caucuses, and without obligating themselves to donors or political parties.

The most radical approach to making the final selection

would be to eliminate the expensive and lengthy general election, choosing a winner by random selection from a slate of carefully vetted candidates, letting luck decide the outcome. That's similar to the way many government positions were filled in ancient Athens. Citizens readily agreed to serve, because service in government was considered as great an honor and duty as service in the military.

Objections I have heard to eliminating competitive elections often come from people who simply can't imagine not voting, especially African-Americans who, after having struggled for so long for the right to vote, may not want to give it up. Fair enough. But let's still allow ourselves to think creatively about all the options.

A less radical approach would be to have the nominating process live-streamed and recorded for the public to review, along with the resumes, testimonials and, as appropriate, personal tax returns provided by the candidates. The public could vote after a couple of weeks, choosing from a qualified list of candidates, but leaving donors, political parties and interminably long campaigns on the trash heap of history.

Choosing a President Without An Election

In the 45 U.S. presidential elections, five presidents have won with less than a majority. More than 10 percent of the time, the majority wanted someone else to be president. It happened most recently in 2000 and again in 2016. The problem rests squarely with the Electoral College—the world's quirkiest institution for choosing the leader of a democratic republic. We're the only democracy that has one.

The founders of our republic didn't trust the uneducated American people, fearing the tyranny of the mob. Instead, they created a system in which each state decides how to pick delegates to an Electoral College, which meets separately in each state, tallying their votes on a national basis to select the president and vice-president. The founders assumed that Electoral College delegates would be more thoughtful and well-informed than the citizenry.

But it hasn't worked that way, because political parties pick the delegates and pledge them to specific candidates. For many years, party leaders in each state told delegates, who were often beholden to the party for their patronage jobs in state government, how they should vote.

We have tried to reform that process through primary elections and caucuses, which are supposed to let citizens— instead of political party bosses—select candidates. But the reforms have had unintended consequences. Barely 20 percent of voters turn up for the primaries[70] and caucuses—but those voters

have more partisan views than the general public. That encourages presidential candidates to lie, saying one thing while running for their party's nomination and then, pivoting, to say something different in the general election.

The election process has become a two-year marathon, with more than two billion dollars spent[71] in each of the last two presidential elections. The need to raise huge sums of money makes candidates beholden to wealthy donors.

In his farewell address in 1796,[72] George Washington warned that the political party, which arose at the outset of the republic for the sole purpose of winning elections, "serves always to distract the public councils and enfeeble the public administration. It agitates the community with ill-founded jealousies and false alarms, kindles the animosity of one part against another, foments occasionally riot and insurrection."

In light of Russia's interference in the 2016 presidential election, you have to wonder if Washington had a crystal ball to foretell the future. He said that the political party "opens the door to foreign influence and corruption, which finds a facilitated access to the government itself through the channels of party passions."

What if, instead of obstructing the people's will, the Electoral College became a truly representative forum for citizens from each state to thoughtfully select the president and vice president, as the founders intended? What if we borrowed an idea from the original Athenian democracy, which selected the majority of its public officials by lottery, like American courts select jurors?

Electoral College delegates would be randomly selected from each state and congressional district and the District of Columbia. This process requires absolutely no change in the

U.S. Constitution, which doesn't prescribe the method for selecting delegates.[73] It could be implemented by changing the selection process on a state-by-state basis. Political parties at a state level now control the rules for selecting Electors. That could be taken out of their hands.

Supported by appropriate staff, the Electors could interview presidential candidates who might be recommended by the Senate, House, state legislatures and citizen petitions, selecting the president and vice president without a national election.

The process would be very transparent, televised over a period of weeks, perhaps with each presidential candidate presenting her or himself in a public interview, accompanied by testimony from others, letters of reference, background reports and the candidates' federal tax returns.

There would be no need for circus-like debates. After all, when in real life do presidents ever appear in such debates after they are elected, except during their election campaign for a second term?

Based on the U.S. Constitution, Electors convene in their respective states, with the possibility that the advent of virtual meeting technology[74] could facilitate a more unified and coordinated event, live-streamed for public viewing. This approach remedies the dilemma that ordinary citizens simply don't have the time nor the facts to make informed decisions amidst their busy lives. But in the right context—with enough time to think and reflect, with balanced information—a group of 538 ordinary citizens, statistically guaranteed by sortition to truly represent their fellow Americans, would likely make a far more thoughtful decision through deliberation than through the current partisan election process.

Perhaps the Electoral College, that quirky institution, unique to America, can finally fulfill its original purpose.

CHAPTER 6

The Pursuit of Power

Power

Human beings all want power. From our first cry as babies, we demand power. "Waaaaaah! I want what I want, and I want it now!"

Most of us want limited power, merely the power to meet our own needs and to have control over our own lives. Some of us, however, want to have power over others. And some of us can't get enough of it.

Most professional politicians are drawn to power like moths to a flame. Lord John-Dahlberg Acton,[75] English historian, politician and writer, in 1887 warned that, "Power tends to corrupt and absolute power corrupts absolutely. Great men are almost always bad men..."

Whew, when I first read that last sentence, I had to think about it for a while.

Power can be used for good purposes, of course, and often is. But for most politicians the priority is getting re-elected, and good causes are all too often sacrificed in the interest of winning.

As far as I know, the first person to assert that "politics is the pursuit of power" was Niccolo Machiavelli,[76] in his famous book *The Prince,* a cynical primer for rulers in the early 1500s. Before Machiavelli, the definition of politics was more benign, referring to governance in general. But Machiavelli explored the darker side of politics, including the strategic use of war to gain power.

No one has expressed a more sinister view of politics than Mao Zedong,[77] the revolutionary who founded Communist China. He said, "Politics is war without bloodshed, while war is politics with bloodshed."

Ironically, Lee Atwater,[78] who at 38 was the youngest man ever to chair the Republican National Committee, perhaps unknowingly employed Mao's definition. He called his work "political warfare" and was a pioneer in negative attack ads. He saw race-baiting as an acceptable campaign strategy.

Sadly, Atwater died of cancer at 40. He expressed his regrets as he prepared to meet his maker, writing one of the most poignant apologies I have ever read (which I will share below).

From Political Governance to Deliberative Governance

My "Building a New Reality" website[79] defines what I call the six facets of a new reality: learning, governance, care, justice, enterprise and spirit. Although my six facets diagram[80] presents them clockwise in that order, the sequence is irrelevant. They are simply a listing of basic needs essential to any functioning society.

However, to paraphrase Tolkien's *Lord of the Rings,*[81] governance[82] is the "one facet to rule them all." To make the transition from political governance to deliberative governance, which is my proposed goal, the pursuit of power is replaced by the pursuit of truth. Under our current system of political governance, power and truth are opposites.

A friend of mine, who serves as chairman of the board of a regional bank, once skeptically asked me if I was trying to change human nature.[83] It's a good question. But no, I'm not trying to change human nature. Too often, we see our frailties and faults as human nature, but I see it differently.

In every moment of our existence we have choices to make, as in the cartoonish image of a devil on one shoulder and an angel on the other, each imploring us to come their way. Human nature is dynamic. We can always choose to succumb to the dark side, and each of us occasionally does. But we also can choose to move toward the light. I see human nature and human history as the struggle between the two.

Given what we have come to know about power, human beings are least likely to be corrupted and drawn to the dark side in a society where we decentralize and share power widely. That is the fundamental thesis of this manifesto.[84]

Authority and Influence

Authority[85] is the official side of governance. Authority is inherent in those who have formal decision-making roles, from parents to presidents.

Influence[86] is the unofficial side of governance. Even the strictest parents and the most powerful dictators must contend with influence, the inherent ability of their children and their citizens to support or defy authority, and to influence others to do the same.

Governance works best in any setting where authority and influence are aligned in support of shared goals. That's what democratic elections are supposed to achieve: Citizens exercise their influence by voting into positions of authority the decision-makers who share their goals.

Sadly, the vast majority of citizens in democratic republics around the world no longer believe that is true.[87] However, we can realign influence and authority by decentralizing governance; allowing people more voice and more choice, in exchange for taking more responsibility.

Selecting legislators by sortition means that citizens do not merely vote for decision-makers. They become the decision-makers.

Influence merges with authority.

The Failure of Political Governance

In 1991, Lee Atwater,[88] Republican National Committee Chairman and a pioneer in political attack ads, was dying from a brain tumor.

Years earlier, in an off-the-record interview that wasn't released until after his death, Atwater explained the so-called "Southern strategy." This allowed Republicans to win the votes of racists without sounding racist themselves—by making the racial messages abstract. Atwater said, "You start out in 1954 by saying, 'Nigger, nigger, nigger.'[89] By 1968 you can't say 'nigger'—that hurts you, backfires. So you say stuff like forced busing, states' rights, and all that stuff..."

Atwater devised the famous attack ad for the 1988 presidential campaign[90] that blamed candidate Michael Dukakis,[91] governor of Massachusetts, for the rape and assault of a white couple by Willie Horton. He was a black convicted murderer who escaped from a weekend release program run by the Massachusetts prison system. Atwater said of Dukakis that he "would strip the bark off the little bastard" and "make Willie Horton his running mate." Ironically, the attack ad blamed Dukakis for a prison program that had been initiated by his predecessor, a Republican governor.

On another occasion, Atwater planted a fake reporter at a press conference to embarrass a Congressional candidate by asking him about his teenage struggle with depression.

Atwater called his work "political warfare." But political warfare drives out good people who don't want to harm others nor be harmed—so they abandon public service to those with thicker skins and harder hearts. Sadly, voters around the world have come to believe that political party warfare is a necessary evil in selecting public officials—a method that might best be called "selection by combat."

Political parties were invented for the purpose of winning elections. George Washington, the first American president, predicted in his farewell address[92] that political parties "are likely, in the course of time and things, to become potent engines, by which cunning, ambitious, and unprincipled men will be enabled to subvert the power of the people and to usurp for themselves the reins of government."

Facing death at only 40 years old, Atwater sought spiritual peace, writing apology letters to Dukakis and other victims of his political dirty tricks. In a final article for Life magazine a month before he died, Lee Atwater wrote: "My illness helped me to see that what was missing in society is what was missing in me: A little heart. A lot of brotherhood..."

"I acquired more wealth, power, and prestige than most. But you can acquire all you want and still feel empty...It took a deadly illness to put me eye to eye with that truth, but it is a truth that the country, caught up in its ruthless ambitions and moral decay, can learn on my dime. I don't know who will lead us...but they must be made to speak to this spiritual vacuum at the heart of American society, this tumor of the soul."

The Potential of Deliberative Governance[93]

Texas is famous for its divisive politics. Moderates are seen by many as spineless. Texas populist Jim Hightower[94] says that in his state "there's nothing in the middle of the road but yellow stripes and dead armadillos."[95]

So how is it possible that Texas, one of the original gas and oil states, is now the nation's leader in renewable energy? How is possible that both conservatives and liberals support this development? What about the dead armadillos?

What transformed the usual partisan political battle between environmentalists and the energy industry was "Deliberative Polling."

From 1996-1998, eight Texas electric utilities asked James Fishkin, then at the University of Texas in Austin, to survey their customers' views on energy options: renewable energy, energy conservation and the related costs. The Deliberative Polls had remarkable credibility, because participants were selected by lottery from the target population—in this case making each deliberative group truly representative of the eight companies' customers.

The results of the Texas energy polls shocked everyone. Texans—from the gas and oil state, who drive more miles in more pickup trucks and SUVs than folks in any other state—were willing to pay extra money for renewable energy and for energy conservation. From an initial telephone poll to the final poll after the deliberation, customer willingness to pay extra money jumped 30 percent, to 84 percent for renewable energy and 73 percent for energy conservation.

Fishkin reports that, after hearing speakers and deliberating with others, people change their choices from the first telephone poll almost seventy percent of the time, a surprising result because, according to empirical research[96] and conventional wisdom, people usually are more resistant to change.

The influence of a Deliberative Poll relies heavily on its legitimacy, enhanced by the meticulous care that the pollsters take to reach agreement with all contending parties in preparing the briefing book. For a Deliberative Poll in Australia, Fishkin and his colleagues did 19 versions of the briefing book until all parties finally agreed that it was fair. All parties trust a process in which they have meaningful voice, and when their concerns are acknowledged.

The Texas electric power industry and the Texas government were deeply influenced by the unexpected results and acted accordingly. In 1996-1998, when the polls were conducted, Texas, the gas and oil state, was 49th of the 50 United States in renewable energy production. Today, Texas is number one.

Power to the people.

CHAPTER 7

The True Representation Pledge

What if we were to demand that every candidate for President, Senate and House of Representatives sign a True Representation Pledge? The pledge strategy can be used in any election, in any country, at the national, state, provincial or local level; wherever people want to demonstrate the potential of sortition and citizens' assemblies, by targeting an important issue that politicians cannot resolve.

In signing the pledge, each candidate would promise, upon being elected to office, that:

. they would quickly enact legislation to authorize and fund a national (or state, provincial or local) citizens' assembly to decide an important issue, identified for the pledge.

. the citizens' assembly would be conducted with a briefing book prepared to fairly represent the pros and cons of a wide range of views on the chosen issue.

. in the case of a U.S. citizens' assembly, for example, 435 American citizens, one from each Congressional district, would be selected by sortition.

. funding would cover the selection process and each delegate's expenses.

. funding would provide staff to support the process and the drafting of a law to reflect the assembly's decisions.

. funding would cover the cost of a venue and live-streaming so that the public can view the deliberative process.

. each Senator, Representative and the President (or relevant elected officials and candidates in other jurisdictions) would wholly support and promptly enact whatever decisions are made by this truly representative group of their fellow citizens.

Why do we think this True Representation Pledge strategy will work?

How The Flaw in Elections Foisted Prohibition on America

In 1920, on the first day of Prohibition,[97] people must have looked around and thought, "How the hell did this happen?"

Wayne Wheeler,[98] leader of the National Anti-Saloon League, knew exactly how it happened. He got America to give up its booze and shut down its fifth-biggest industry by exploiting the flaw at the center of the election process—the gap between winning and losing.

He boasted that he did it the way the political party bosses did it. He built loyalty among a unified bloc of voters who, although a small minority, could control a close election. Any candidate with 45 percent of the electorate could win with the help of the league's voting bloc. But if the candidate refused to support Prohibition, Wheeler would have the bloc shift its votes to the opponent.

In 1903, the League decided to oppose 70 Ohio legislators and defeated every one of them. In 1905, the League challenged the Ohio governor who had previously been elected with the largest plurality in state history. Although Republicans won every other statewide race in Ohio, the Republican governor was defeated and his political career ruined. The League's display of power in Ohio allowed it to intimidate politicians in every state, until Prohibition was enacted at a national level through an amendment to the U.S. Constitution.

What Wayne Wheeler perfected was a strategy that allows a small group of single-issue voters to impose its will on the rest of the nation. What if we were to use Wayne Wheeler's strategy to save democracies everywhere, at every level of government, from their current partisan quagmire?

Those of us who want to explore the possibility of a more deliberative democracy can exploit the flaw in elections, in the same way that Wayne Wheeler pressured legislators to support his cause. With only a small percentage of determined voters, we can decide any close election in favor of candidates who agree to take to take the True Representation Pledge.

The True Representation Petition

First, we must launch a petition drive to secure enough voter signatures to pose a credible threat to politicians who resist signing. We don't have to change governments or constitutions to take the first step. We just have to get candidates to agree to voluntarily delegate their authority and enact legislation that provides adequate funding for the expenses of conducting and live-streaming a citizens' assembly, and subsequently honor the assembly's decisions by voting them into law.

As the number of names on the petition grows, the threat will become more credible. If candidates agree to support us, they can use our True Representation logo on their campaign literature and websites. A successful True Representation effort will pave the way for future citizens' assemblies to deal with other controversial issues that politicians are afraid to tackle.

This is a pragmatic first step. We're not proposing a permanent change in government. Rather, we want to give people around the globe a chance to see how sortition and participatory decision-making can work in practice.

Ending James Madison's American Nightmare

James Madison trusted the American people to a point, but he worried about when they became a mob. He wanted to find a way to slow things down when that happened, creating mechanisms for calm deliberation. He had envisioned a Senate chosen by state legislatures, not by direct election, and an Electoral College that chose the President, instead of voters. But it hasn't worked out the way that he hoped. Yet the use of citizens' assemblies chosen by sortition, an old idea in a modern context, will create a deliberative process absolutely consistent with the intentions of Madison and the other founders.

When Benjamin Franklin emerged from the Constitutional Convention in 1787 and was asked what kind of government was proposed, he said, "A republic, if you can keep it."

He was talking to us. And so was John F. Kennedy, when he urged us to ask what we can do for our country. His words touched my fourteen-year-old spirit. I have since grown to understand that if we want more voice and choice, which is the promise of democracy, then we must take more responsibility.

Perhaps Americans can set an example and inspire others, as we have done in the past, to overcome adversity and embrace a renewed spirit of democracy.

One might question whether the proposed reform—sortition rather than election—is relevant to America, because it was developed in ancient Athens; an imperfect democracy in which men without property, women and slaves were not allowed to participate. But that exactly matches the American democracy of Franklin's time—men without property, women and slaves were not allowed to participate.

However, in the two centuries since the founding of the American republic, we have evolved. We can continue to do so.

We must.

ADDENDUM

Recommended Resources on Citizens' Assemblies and Sortition

Books

Democracy When the People Are Thinking: Revitalizing Our Politics Through Public Deliberation (James S. Fishkin, 2018)

Democracy requires a connection to the "will of the people." What does that mean in a world of "fake news," relentless advocacy, dialogue mostly among the like-minded, and massive spending to manipulate public opinion? What kind of opinion can the public have under such conditions? What would democracy be like if the people were really thinking in depth about the policies they must live with? If they really "deliberated" with good information about their political choices?

The End of Politicians: Time for a Real Democracy (Brett Hennig, 2017)
Our politics is broken, but it can be fixed. A real democracy is not only possible—it is an urgent necessity. Provocative, succinct and inspiring, The End of Politicians combines insights from the history of democracy with a critical understanding of the information revolution to explain how we can fix democracy, by eliminating politicians and replacing them with a representative network of everyday citizens *(Source: Goodreads).*

The Wisdom of Crowds: Why the Many Are Smarter Than the Few and How Collective Wisdom Shapes Business, Economies, Societies and Nations (James Surowiecki, 2004)
In this fascinating book, former New Yorker business columnist James Surowiecki explores a deceptively simple idea: Large groups of people are smarter than an elite few, no matter how brilliant; better at solving problems, fostering innovation, coming to wise decisions, even predicting the future. With boundless erudition and in delightfully clear prose, Surowiecki ranges across fields as diverse as popular culture, psychology, ant biology, behavioral economics, artificial intelligence, military history, and politics, to show how this simple idea offers important lessons for how we live our lives, select our leaders, run our companies, and think about our world.

Articles

The Case for Governing by Lottery[99] in the *Boston Globe* (Alex Guerrero, 2012)
The Lottocracy[100] at Aeon website (Alex Guerrero, 2014)
Both of these articles offer an excellent explanation of Guerrero's idea of Lottocracy. For those who don't have access to a university library, reading these are a useful alternative to paying a fee to read the original academic journal article[101]: *Against Elections: The Lottocratic Alternative* (2014).

The Nation in a Room[102] at *Boston Review* website (James S. Fishkin, 2006)
An excellent article by Fishkin that explains Deliberative Polling by contrasting it with George Gallup's vision of national public policy polling.

Videos

By The People: What's Next California?[103] (57 minutes)
Hosted by The PBS NewsHour's Judy Woodruff, *By The People: What's Next California?* follows the gathering of a representative sample of 412 registered California voters in Torrance, for the state's first-ever Deliberative Poll in June, 2011. Weekend discussions and results of the before-and-after poll on key issues facing the state were captured and are presented for viewers.

When Citizens Assemble[104] (17 minutes)
This film by Patrick Chalmers succinctly explains how Ireland's efforts to break a political deadlock over its de facto ban on abortion was an inspired and bold response—the creation of a Citizens' Assembly to tackle the issue. During five weekends spread over five months, a random selection of Irish people deliberated on the highly divisive and controversial issue. Subsequently, the Irish people used the Assembly's decisions as the basis for a nationwide referendum, which eliminated the comprehensive ban. The Assembly represents a breakthrough moment, not just for Ireland, but also for ways of doing politics in the rest of the world. By using random selection and deliberation to seek solutions to a highly contentious issue, rather than leaving it to elected politicians, Ireland has gifted us all a real-life lesson in doing democracy differently.

What If We Replaced Politicians With Randomly Selected People?[105]
(TED Talk, 10 minutes)
If you think democracy is broken, let's replace politicians with randomly selected people. Author and activist Brett Hennig presents a compelling case for sortition democracy, or random selection of government officials—a system with roots in ancient Athens, that taps into the wisdom of the crowd and entrusts ordinary people with making balanced decisions for the greater good of everyone. Sound crazy? Learn more about how it could work to create a world free of partisan politics.

Websites

Building a New Reality[106] is my own website. It provides an overview of the six facets of a new reality, including "the one facet to rule them all," governance. There is a series of blog posts by several authors, including myself, on Citizens' Assemblies[107] and a growing number of posts and pages on our True Representation[108] Pledge campaign to change the U.S. political democracy to a deliberative democracy.

Sortition Foundation[109] offers resources about sortition-selected legislatures, citizens' assemblies, and the campaign for a U.K. Citizens' House to replace the House of Lords.

Center for Deliberative Democracy[110] at Stanford University has a wealth of information on more than two decades of Deliberative Polling,™ including a timeline and description of more than 100 deliberative polls.

A U.S. Citizens' Assembly on Gun Control

The strategy used by Wayne Wheeler of the National Anti-Saloon League to impose the "Prohibition" of alcoholic beverages on the rest of the nation in 1920 is the same strategy used by the National Rifle Association (NRA)[111] to avoid even a meaningful discussion of the pros and cons of gun control.

Both organizations demonstrated how a small, determined minority can achieve its goals by exploiting the vulnerability of politicians in our flawed competitive election system.

I propose using that same single-issue strategy to bring about a U.S. Citizens' Assembly on Gun Control, a participatory approach to one of our nation's most challenging issues: how to limit gun violence in America.

Please understand that I am not promoting any particular position on gun control. Whether your view is to totally resist any restrictions on guns or totally abolish guns, or more likely, if your views fall somewhere in between, why can't Americans have a thoughtful, deliberative process about one of our most challenging issues?

(In the interest of transparency, if you'd like to know my personal view on gun control, read my "Building A New Reality"[112] website blogpost entitled "The Good Old NRA."[113])

In the first chapter of my 1992 book, The Electronic Congress,[114] I wrote, "The NRA opposes all gun control legislation, although 87 percent of American gun owners, according to a 1989 Time/CNN Poll, favor a federal law requiring a seven-day waiting period and a background check for anyone who wants to buy a handgun."

In 1993, The Brady Handgun Violence Prevention Act[115] was passed, named after White House press secretary James Brady, who was shot and disabled in the 1981 attempted assassination of President Ronald Reagan. The law required background checks before a gun is purchased from a licensed dealer, manufacturer or importer. Since then, critics on both sides of the gun control issue have argued that the law is ineffectual,[116] but for different reasons.

In 1994, an assault weapons ban was imposed[117]—a temporary prohibition in effect from September of 1994 to

September of 2004. Multiple attempts to renew the ban have failed, despite the fact that 70% of the public in 2018[118] favored restoring the ban.

I find it deeply distressing that the gun violence issue I wrote about in 1992 is still challenging us today. Whatever the solution, we can't solve anything by doing nothing.

My friend David Heekin is one of the contributors to my Building A New Reality website.[119] I may not agree with him at times, but I always find him open to genuine discussion. In an article he wrote for his own Facebook page, entitled "Evolution of a Gunslinger," he described his take on the current impasse on gun control:

> The AR-15 has been in the news a lot lately. In case you've been living on Mars and have not heard, the AR-15 is the civilian version of the military's M-16/M4 primary infantry weapon. A group of uncompromising fanatics insists that it is an assault weapon and should be banned. Another group of uncompromising fanatics shrills that it is most definitely NOT an assault weapon, and insists that any attempt to ban the AR-15 is an assault on the 2nd Amendment to the Bill of Rights, the Constitution of the United States and their individual rights as citizens thereof. No negotiating, no compromise, no quarter asked or offered, and no prisoners taken by either side.

No matter where you stand on gun control, you will likely agree that being stubborn and shouting the same arguments at each other is futile. It's time to move beyond the impasse—but we need your help.

If you're waiting for politicians and our dysfunctional political system to solve our problems, you will first die of old age. Instead, we're proposing a public deliberation by a truly representative group of ordinary Americans—an approach that has the potential to reinvigorate our democracy and get something meaningful accomplished at the same time.

Subscribe now[120] to get weekly updates and blogs. We'll keep you posted as we move forward.

Achieving more voice and more choice requires that we take more shared responsibility.

Join us.

Chapter Notes

1. What To Do For Your Country

1. https://commons.wikimedia.org/wiki/File:1960_-_John_Kennedy_at_Center_Square_-_Allentown_PA.jpg
2. https://en.wikipedia.org/wiki/Mayors_of_Allentown,_Pennsylvania#/media/File:1964_-_John_T_Gross.jpg
3. https://en.wikipedia.org/wiki/George_McGovern_1972_presidential_campaign
4. https://en.wikipedia.org/wiki/Yankee_Doodle
5. https://www.tedwachtel.com/?page_id=46
6. https://en.wikipedia.org/wiki/Buckminster_Fuller
7. https://www.tedwachtel.com/?page_id=118
8. http://bostonreview.net/archives/BR31.2/fishkin.php

2. The Myth of Voting

9. https://www.aclu.org/issues/voting-rights
10. https://en.wikipedia.org/wiki/Athenian_democracy
11. https://en.wikipedia.org/wiki/Sortition
12. https://en.wikipedia.org/wiki/Kleroterion
13. http://bostonreview.net/archives/BR31.2/fishkin.php
14. https://en.wikipedia.org/wiki/Politics_(Aristotle)
15. https://en.wikipedia.org/wiki/Kim_Jong-un
16. http://founding.com/prudence-indeed-will-dictate-that-governments-long-established-should-not-be-changed-for-light-and-transient-causes

17. https://www.statista.com/statistics/300427/eu-parlament-turn-out-for-the-european-elections
18. https://www.idea.int/sites/default/files/publications/voter-turnout-trends-around-the-world.pdf
19. https://www.transparency.org/gcb2013
20. http://www.people-press.org/2015/11/23/1-trust-in-government-1958-2015
21. https://www.mountvernon.org/library/digitalhistory/digital-encyclopedia/article/elizabeth-willing-powel
22. https://en.wikipedia.org/wiki/Manifesto
23. https://en.wikipedia.org/wiki/Citizens%27_assembly
24. https://en.wikipedia.org/wiki/James_S._Fishkin
25. https://cdd.stanford.edu
26. http://cdd.stanford.edu/1998/deliberative-polling-texas-electric-utilities
27. https://www.youtube.com/watch?v=k5cpY0MuMDU
28. https://www.sortitionfoundation.org
29. https://en.wikipedia.org/wiki/House_of_Lords
30. https://en.wikipedia.org/wiki/House_of_Commons
31. https://www.bretthennig.com/about
32. https://en.wikipedia.org/wiki/Citizens%27_assembly
33. http://www.g1000.org/en
34. https://www.buildinganewreality.com/the-irish-citizens-assembly-chooses-representatives-by-lottery-not-election
35. https://www.buildinganewreality.com
36. https://www.citizensassembly.ie/en
37. https://www.youtube.com/watch?v=MjpuDk9_BWI
38. https://www.resilience.org/stories/2017-11-22/solutions-how-the-poles-are-making-democracy-work-again-in-gdansk/
39. https://en.wikipedia.org/wiki/Pawe%C5%82_Adamowicz
40. https://www.amazon.com/dp/1911586106

3. The Wisdom of Crowds

41. https://en.wikipedia.org/wiki/James_Surowiecki
42. https://en.wikipedia.org/wiki/The_Wisdom_of_Crowds
43. https://en.wikipedia.org/wiki/Francis_Galton
44. https://www.archives.gov/electoral-college/about
45. https://en.wikipedia.org/wiki/Jeffrey_Rosen_(academic)
46. https://www.montpelier.org/learn/the-life-of-james-madison
47. https://history.state.gov/milestones/1784-1800/convention-and-ratification

48. https://www.monticello.org/site/research-and-collections/
     senatorial-saucer
49. https://www.theatlantic.com/magazine/archive/2018/10/
     james-madison-mob-rule/568351
50. https://www.investopedia.com/terms/i/indexfund.asp
51. https://en.wikipedia.org/wiki/2000_United_States_presidential_
     election_recount_in_Florida#Palm_Beach_County's_butterfly_ballots
52. https://en.wikipedia.org/wiki/Fake_news
53. https://www.custominsight.com/articles/random-sampling.asp
54. https://public.tableau.com/profile/zach.roberts#!/vizhome/
     SortitionSenators/Both

4. The Nation in a Room

55. https://www.gallup.com/corporate/178136/george-gallup.aspx
56. https://psycnet.apa.org/record/1940-04662-000
57. https://en.wikipedia.org/wiki/James_S._Fishkin
58. http://bostonreview.net/archives/BR31.2/fishkin.php
59. https://www.amazon.com/Democracy-When-People-Are-Thinking-
     ebook/dp/B07F37Y736
60. https://news.gallup.com/poll/1600/congress-public.aspx
61. https://wagner.nyu.edu/files/admissions/mayer.realignment.pdf
62. https://en.wikipedia.org/wiki/Gun_control
63. https://www.nytimes.com/2016/01/09/opinion/steve-israel-
     confessions-of-a-congressman.html

5. The Sortition Menu

64. http://www.alexguerrero.org
65. https://onlinelibrary.wiley.com/doi/abs/10.1111/papa.12029
66. https://aeon.co/essays/forget-voting-it-s-time-to-start-choosing-our-
     leaders-by-lottery
67. http://fortune.com/2017/12/04/republican-tax-bill-donors
68. https://www.buildinganewreality.com/series/citizens-assemblies/
69. https://people.howstuffworks.com/jury-duty-summons.htm
70. https://bipartisanpolicy.org/blog/2018-primary-election-results
71. https://www.washingtonpost.com/news/wonk/wp/2017/04/14/
     somebody-just-put-a-price-tag-on-the-2016-election-its-a-doozy
72. http://avalon.law.yale.edu/18th_century/washing.asp
73. https://www.usconstitution.net/consttop_elec.html
74. https://en.wikipedia.org/wiki/Web_conferencing

6. The Pursuit of Power

75. https://en.wikipedia.org/wiki/John_Dalberg-Acton,_1st_Baron_ Acton
76. https://en.wikipedia.org/wiki/Niccol%C3%B2_Machiavelli
77. https://en.wikiquote.org/wiki/Mao_Zedong
78. https://en.wikipedia.org/wiki/Lee_Atwater
79. https://www.buildinganewreality.com
80. https://www.buildinganewreality.com/the-six-facets
81. https://www.amazon.com/dp/B007978OY6
82. https://www.buildinganewreality.com/governance
83. https://en.wikipedia.org/wiki/Human_nature
84. https://en.wikipedia.org/wiki/Manifesto
85. https://en.wikipedia.org/wiki/Authority
86. https://en.wikipedia.org/wiki/Influence
87. https://www.transparency.org/gcb2013
88. https://en.wikipedia.org/wiki/Lee_Atwater
89. https://www.thenation.com/article/exclusive-lee-atwaters-infamous-1981-interview-southern-strategy
90. https://www.cnn.com/2018/11/01/politics/willie-horton-ad-1988-explainer-trnd/index.html
91. https://en.wikipedia.org/wiki/Michael_Dukakis
92. http://avalon.law.yale.edu/18th_century/washing.asp
93. https://en.wikipedia.org/wiki/Deliberative_democracy
94. https://en.wikipedia.org/wiki/Jim_Hightower
95. https://www.amazon.com/dp/B0046XSKKY
96. https://www.newyorker.com/magazine/2017/02/27/why-facts-dont-change-our-minds

7. The True Representation Pledge

97. https://www.britannica.com/event/Prohibition-United-States-history-1920-1933
98. https://en.wikipedia.org/wiki/Wayne_Wheeler

Addendum: Recommended Resources

Articles

99. https://www.bostonglobe.com/ideas/2012/12/02/the-case-for-governing-lottery/ALeFzJbT836BmRjoPMwQtJ/story.html
100. https://aeon.co/essays/forget-voting-it-s-time-to-start-choosing-our-leaders-by-lottery

101. https://onlinelibrary.wiley.com/doi/pdf/10.1111/papa.12029
102. http://bostonreview.net/james-fishkin-nation-in-a-room-turning-public-opinion-into-policy

Videos
103. https://www.youtube.com/watch?v=k5cpY0MuMDU
104. https://www.youtube.com/watch?v=MjpuDk9_BWI
105. https://www.ted.com/talks/brett_hennig_what_if_we_replaced_politicians_with_randomly_selected_people?language=en

Websites
106. https://www.buildinganewreality.com
107. https://www.buildinganewreality.com/series-citizens-assemblies/ 108. https://www.buildinganewreality.com/true-representation/
109. https://www.sortitionfoundation.org/
110. https://cdd.stanford.edu/

A Call to Action
111. https://en.wikipedia.org/wiki/National_Rifle_Association
112. https://www.buildinganewreality.com/
113. https://www.buildinganewreality.com/the-good-old-nra/
114. https://www.tedwachtel.com/?page_id=46
115. https://en.wikipedia.org/wiki/Brady_Handgun_Violence_Prevention_Act
116. https://en.wikipedia.org/wiki/Gun_control
117. https://en.wikipedia.org/wiki/Federal_Assault_Weapons_Ban
118. https://www.businessinsider.com/assault-weapons-ban-poll-gun-reform-2018-2
119. https://buildinganewreality.com/staff/
120. https://www.buildinganewreality.com/true-representation/

About the Author

Ted Wachtel is a visionary, an educator and a serial entrepreneur, in that order. He has always seen the world as it could be, in its best potential sense.

A man of action, he worked toward that vision first as an educator in the Pennsylvania public school system. Quickly realizing the limitations of what he came to view as an outmoded system that didn't adequately serve all would-be learners, he began working toward a better way; one that addressed the needs of learners who hadn't been able to thrive in the rigid, traditional classroom structure.

From there, he and Susan, his wife, launched a series of projects; some short-lived, but most ongoing. They have organized local political campaigns, founded schools, group homes, counseling and treatment programs for adolescents, an accredited master's degree-granting graduate school, an art museum, a solar housing development, an organic mini-farm, a food cooperative, a book publishing company and more, mostly in the United States but also several projects overseas.

In service of many of these goals, Ted wrote or co-wrote many books, and continues to do so today. Despite having officially retired in 2015, he shows no signs of slowing down his energetic pace, though he does now take more time to spend with loved ones and enjoying the fruits of his many and varied labors over the years.

Building a New Reality is a non-partisan, evidence-based social movement dedicated to the decentralization of power and to participatory decision-making in every facet of society: learning, governance, care, justice, enterprise and spirit.

We advocate for more voice and more choice, in exchange for taking more responsibility.

True Representation is the key goal of representative governance—the bullseye of democracy.

Visit our website and look around. You can subscribe at the bottom of any page to get blogposts and updates.

Join us.

NOTES

NOTES

NOTES

NOTES

NOTES

NOTES

NOTES

NOTES

NOTES

Made in the USA
Columbia, SC
11 August 2020

15224829R00054